CU00519221

Life After Life After Death

Manchester-born, Oxford-bred, Felix Hodcroft gained degrees in English Literature and Applied Social Sciences. He worked as a probation officer in Birmingham, Hull and East Yorkshire, but since 2010 has devoted more of his time to poetry. He has also written a novel for children, *Lives of Lilo*, published by Valley Press in 2012.

Studying, writing and performing poetry have been major factors in what limited success he has achieved in straddling life's tangled awfulness and glory; so he's proud to be a member and former Chair of the Scarborough Poetry Workshop.

Life After
Life After Death

FELIX HODCROFT

For Belinda

Thankyou!

Felix xxx
June 2012

VALLEY

LIFE AFTER LIFE AFTER DEATH

First published in 2010 by Valley Press
Second edition 2011
www.valleypressuk.com

Printed in England by Imprint Digital,
Upton Pyne, Exeter

ISBN: 978-0-9568904-9-8
Cat no.: VP0020

A catalogue record for this book
is available from the British Library

www.valleypressuk.com/authors/felixhodcroft

9 8 7 6 5 4 3 2

CONTENTS

To the memory of my friend Chris Woodland,
with admiration, love and thanks.

PART ONE : DEATH

Inside Ros's Head

Meet Ros. She's a
dynamo. Human express train.
Tackles each task
as though it were a virgin and she was a vampire.
Spits out the raw bleeding heart of it.
Rip off the wrapping, the froth and the flavouring,
pinpoint the core, then work outwards.
There's always an answer, incisive, precise.
Except that there isn't, of course.

Finds herself pumping the buttons again and again.
Then starting to bang at the grille with the heel of her shoe
'I hate being shut-in!'
Her eyes might explode or her tongue catch fire,
little things drive her half-crazed.
Somebody biting their nails or
forgetfulness, especially hers.
The panic that slithers beneath every rational day
as she bursts from one underpass,
drills her way into another –

then suddenly slows to a crawl.
Fifteen summers ago, on a sweet breezy night.
Coming home from a wonderful time
with a man who had made her feel beautiful, clever,
and safe; and how many do that?
None since, that's for sure –
and she'd only had four drinks, reactions just
slowed down a bit, not much over the limit,
distracted? Perhaps; something trivial,

parents, relationships, cash, nothing more than a
flash across her vision, thud BANG! as
her foot jerked and fumbled –

'You stop automatically.
Nothing – anywhere – moving.
Found that I'd wet myself. Literally.
Wet myself.
If there'd been any movement, I'd have –
obviously! But nothing – anywhere – so I
what? Changed my knickers, well
always a spare pair – don't you?
Then I managed to stop myself shaking – keep
calm you bitch
CALM! First – this isn't a dream; b)
you can't wind back time; so
drive back into work, to the car park.'

She stops. Her voice deepens and slows.
Incisive, precise,
what you do is find answers.

'Drove my car straight into a pillar, it
folds up like cardboard, carbody,
doesn't it? Crushes out the previous
damage and then it's quite simple.
Woman driver, no sense
of direction manoeuvring;
joke of the office for days.
See, at first I had panicked, but later…'
she smiles, chews her nail –

'I'm not saying it was right but
how would turning myself in
have helped –
I'm talking about the good I've been able –
that I've *made* myself do
for these last fifteen years.
As for not telling anyone –
well, not until you –
I'm proud of it hasn't been easy except…'

Except,
not a day passes that she doesn't hear *thud-
BANG!* Remembers. And shudders.
And as for each knock of the front door
when no one's expected,
each ring of the telephone…
Wakes in a sweat once or twice every month.
But she won't tell you any of this;
or that, deeper within her babooshka nest yet,
the smallest yet fiercest Ros
burns with a sulphuric rage.
Why me? What else could I do?
And what sort of bitch would allow her child out
crossing streets at that hour?

In Ros's head, cogs turn in different directions
on different levels.
As they bite on each other
they drive something mighty,
perpetually bubbling over.
While Ros's soul sits by a river of tears

and waits for the cogs to wind down or
the eyes to explode or the express train
to screech off the rails...

And you?
You don't want to buy her another brandy;
still less, for her to treat you.
Is she sorry she told you?
She senses your horror, your awe and confusion;
those cogs spin round quicker and quicker.

Despatch from the Truth Factories

You'd expected fat fingers jabbing an inch from your eye
and stale breath.
Not this soft voice *tell us your truth!*

After a while, though, they start interrupting,
taking you backwards or forwards and asking for details of
    How did you?
What did you think that you thought that you wanted and why?
An hour or two, you'll get weary,
confused what they've got, what they want.
Uncertain what time it is, hungry,
a teeny bit anxiously twitchful.
They do anxiously awfully well.
It's something about the way that their smiles click on-off,
then back on; then back off.
You won't tell us?
Look, we'll make it up anyway and no one will care.
As they scrape their chairs closer and closer.

Now you'll see what their loved ones don't.
How to rip open tight packaging;
how to stamp on the sweets;
the sleeve up the backside, the wind up and jerk on the
    rope's end till –

this storm passes too.
Generously now, they'll explain *you've*
been put through our wringer but mate
you've held firm and that
proves we've been wrong all along, so

come on – cigarette? cup of tea? And
let's get it on record, told your way –
official account!

Which makes you feel suddenly grateful and tearful,
'cause it's true it's pretty amazing how dogged you've been!
And oh!
the relief as at long last you tell them it straight
and they smile and they nod,
they don't challenge or quibble and
finally you run out of words.
And there's silence.
And then one of them sighs and says
right, that's a start…

And you say *look hang on, I was straight!*
And they laugh *you? You can't even piss straight!*
And you say *it's not fair!*
And they say to you *fair? What*
exactly has fair got to do with this?
Did you think we were playing some game?

Did you mistake them for archaeologists?
Unearthing, sifting, stroking the truth free
from dirt, lies, confusion?
These are artists and you're not
the landscape, you're paint.
They will spatter the walls with you then,
dipping their quills in your heart,
they will write up their story, not
your story, their story,
theirs.

Good Riddance to Ms Babwe Jones

Saw this girl I used to know, Somebody Jones, being
bundled into a Merc by the man in a charcoal-grey suit and
   big glasses,
the guy she left me for;
thought about running across the road but
got my nose bloodied the last time I did and
so I decided I shouldn't.

Thought I could see, behind the smoked glass,
her scrunched eyes screaming and so I
ducked back into TK Maxx I
didn't want to make things any worse.

But wanted to know where he'd taken her –
lovely girl in those halcyon days when I'd had my hands all
   over her.
So I hailed a taxi and
bowled off down Commonwealth Street on the chase
past the rainbow-hued, frowning-faced, iPod-clad
passers-by on the other side,
while eruptions in the back of the Merc
shattered a quarter window.

This guy she left me for, black like her, well-spoken, bit of a
   thug,
but that's how they are, that's their culture, that's fine and
I'm not one to criticise that.
But a video of her being smacked (always carry a camera –
   don't you?)
might make *someone* do *something* or

at the least I could sell it to one of those
you've been snapped! shows.

And the cabbie was nattering
Looks like they're beating seven bells out of someone and
Why do they keep slowing down so as we can catch up and
Thirty five quid on the meter mate, still up for this?

They might have got guns, I was thinking, of
course I've got a gun – haven't you?
But a mess I might have to explain, is it worth it
just for an old girlfriend's life?
For thirty five quid and some bodies perhaps,
wouldn't *you* want the car – and the petrol of course – and
   the oil –
yes, there's always the oil!
And a couple of charcoal grey suits (bullet hole-
less if poss.) and Calvin Klein watches –
oh trust me, they'd have been wearing them –
and the Merc'd have a stereo, too.
Now *that's* starting to tot up.
But for now, I thought,
better just track 'em.

Out on the marshes
where dogs run in packs, the kites scream and
the estuary winds cut your cheeks,
the Merc stopped, a door belched and
Babwe – yes, that was her name! – Babwe
dived out – or maybe got pushed – face first into the road.
As she lay there, that guy of hers thrust out his backside
and pulled down those smart charcoal trousers

and I thought, though I may have been wrong,
he was pointing his arse back at me –
but might just have been shitting in her face, I don't know,
he might have meant no disrespect.

Then the Merc sped off
and we slowly crunched over the little stones and bones with
the cabbie whistling *Gawd! Look at her trying*
to crawl should we shoot some more film? and
Look mate no offence but I don't want her bleeding up the back of
    my cab
and *Are you gonna phone the cops then?* and
I could just drive up over her head
like I did with this fox that
got hit on the motorway and its back leg half off and –

Shut up! I cried, *let me think!*
Think about options and risks.
She was beautiful, Babwe,
even through the blood and the scabs, tears and filth, but
she didn't seem to clock it was me which was
good for I didn't want her making it
even more difficult to rationally decide what to do and then
Look, I said, *even if we help her – and yes, yes, maybe we should –*
She will only go back again to him or
to somebody else of his sort,
because that's what they do all the time, his sort, her sort,
she's not mine any more, I don't know what it is
they expect me to do and
I'm tired of this, sick, sick to death.
Just drive back to London, I'll call out the police, paramedics
or United Nations

19

for all the difference it'll make in the end.
Anyway,
did you get the Merc's number?

But d'you know what?
And this'll prove just
how upset we both were –
neither of us had written it down.

Song of Those Who Were Saved

To have mislaid so much!
Umbrellas, hearts;
your father, your figure;
those gold summer evenings;
your pep and your patience;
blonde hair.

We never sailed to
the ruined city in the dunes.
Our skiff, at harbour, rocking,
as we stripped, swam, slept.

On a bottomless,
harbourless ocean, we held
even keel on the fierce turquoise swell.
Till, one spice-scented dawn,
simply slipped overboard.

Now dead leaves strew both banks,
our embers fade then fall.
Spring could yet return but for
the rain, this bitter rain that
chills the blood.

Peer through the mist.
Gaze down the well.
Its eye is dark juice,
if you drink, you'll weep.

He knows our look,
our walk, he runs, he
clasps our trembling hands.
He draws us from the bridge's edge,
he tells us we are precious,
he brews us tea and
simply, quietly listens

to the same pattern, same chorus,
year after year,
harvests fail
cancers bloom
men's souls rot.
Weep for what has gone we may,
drink deep of what the cup still holds we
should we surely should but when
the tears have dried the cup is drained,
we must turn and confront
what's still to come.

My Other Daughter

As
I have grown older, so she has grown up.
Sometimes acned and
blasting the ugliest music.
But at my bleak and tangled times,
slim, heart-stoppingly lovely.

Sometimes
I've noticed her watching, from behind a streetlight,
my children and me as we walk, as
we laugh through the dripping dusk.
Closing the plump, warm curtains,
I've glimpsed her dark shadow and
felt guilt rip at my bowels.
But then she'll smile,
raise her hand and
slowly waggle her fingers –
Hiya Mum!

Sometimes,
she weeps for the ripe morning air
on her face, first width of the baths,
all of the candles in one birthday breath.
All of the things I forbade her.
But if
my face is wet I tell myself it's
with kisses, her kisses, for sparing her –
what?
An unready mother, an unwilling father –
no love, patience, money or hope.

She
would have been rather beautiful I think but
of course might have had her father's thin lips or
my bottle legs yet
never does in my dreams.
She would, I think, have been smart.
But might have died in her cot, a climbing frame fall or
a screeching, screaming
hit and run.
And I could never have recovered,
the way that I have.

Jelly in the furnace.
She'll never leave my side
until I die.
The others have
already.

Tea at Elliston and Cavell's

In her shabbyish coat, in this starched and posh café,
a middle-aged woman, no longer dazzling,
waits

for the boy who sits slouched in the chalk-silted classroom
and scratches his line after line after line and
stares up

at the clock hand that jerks like an insect that's dying, like
a ceiling descending to crush, thirty years it's
clicked round,

it's so strange how the plainest of tools can sustain
its own idiot function while Babylon rises and
falls,

though the fingers that hung it are arthritis-twisted, the
fingers that carved it are bones caked in clay
and the first

boys it tortured have sons whose own clockwork's already
nudging them nearer and nearer the brink where
time sags and

deflates, while the boy hurls his pencil down, rips up
his papers and sprints through the echoing playground, his
red satchel

scything through fields of hot shoppers with parched throats
and stale eyes, they need tea, give them cake! at that swish
restaurant

where a woman sits, thinking the love of her life has
forgotten their special treat, off with his mates
or *some girl!*

and she throws down those menus and spoons she's been
   fiddling with,
stumbles past waitresses, out through the one door as
he hurries

in through the other and, being a boy's too
embarrassed to ask, as the minutes wherein
he might catch her drip past, as a nerve in his cheek
begins trembling and she? on a bus
weeps.
She weeps,

this is only one sentence, in one book from thousands
in a library somewhere in Babylon –
so?

So why will this mother and son keep replaying
this misunderstanding, this failure by inches
to meet up for afternoon tea for
the rest of their lives?

Spilled

Returning through the park,
they stumbled into a sea of children
skeltering scrambling,
Kim tried to smile.
But Mark froze.
His face seized up.
The shopping bags he carried
slipped right through his fingers and spilled out.
A giggle of little girls
danced round him like a maypole as,
chest heaving, he started punching at his face.

Mothers looked up sharply.
Just a madman? Or
more dangerous…?
Kim came hurrying back.
'Come on love, it's alright.'
The party swirled around them,
the children oblivious, the adults
just pretending.
Tins and apples rolling underfoot,
Kim kissed Mark's eyes dry,
rubbed his hands.
They started picking up the mess.

On an oceanshore,
where dusk is always falling and
the wind's so piercing, kneels a child.
Alone, all hope dead now
and sobbing without comfort;
but waiting for you,
still.

Knife's Tale

Glossy blade, spotted with blood,
congeals into rust as years pass.
Handle of silvery tongue
whispering away in the darkness.

Someone slashes their fingers
poking into the wainscoting after a mouse.
Lockjaw will follow.
Never my intention.

Ease me out wrapped in a towel.
Rub, scrape and polish me.
Focus for chat at dessert;
look! Applepeel endlessly curling.
But it isn't enough.

She practises lunges and feints in the mirror.
Mimes a kill; finds this excites her.
Scared now, slams me away in a drawer for decades
away from the kiss of fresh air.

Till the lock is picked by her two bereaved sons.
The plain one grabs her paste jewels.
The charming one trousers my dusty gleam but
he couldn't say why.
Not at first.

I'm the blade that slices onions, bread –
then suddenly a windpipe.
Frightening; the choking and clutching!

He hurls me into the sea.
Of course, the tide bears me back, like a fashion,
but he's already filched another for
once used, my loss leaves a hole
big as the person's ambition.

Blunted by salt and sand,
used by peasants for gutting and whittling,
passed to their raucous kids
like a dirty joke
to be spun through the air to hit
soft white bark next to soft naked thighs.

One day someone means it; aims true.
Tasting crimson, I wake I
vibrate to the screams for it's
what I was made for.
To harm.

Kicked and cursed into cobwebby corners.
Rescued each century or so from
a midden or somebody's ribs
poking out from a shallow-dug grave.

Tried and found curious, elegant.
Kept for the thrill, for the power, then
abandoned in panic as
decades like stormclouds roll over me.

And now couched on vellum,
throned behind glass,
morsel of antique debris.

Every few days comes that stare – like hunger.
Fingers that twitch to smash my case
and hand me back to the sunlight
for another few moments, days, deaths.

Take me,
give me the knots in your stomach.
Give me the knots in your life, in your world.
I will sever them

and possibly you.

Final Day of the Last Summer Term

The pock of willow on aggregate.
The dull of the traffic that crosses the old bridge that
spans the river that threads the city.
The gentle applause of trees.

The bowlers kept winding and stamping and hurling but
I kept blocking, nudging and fumbling.
Spectators' bones crumbled
into the long grass, I
snicked my top score, Oh! so proud

as the evening ripened, polished,
the huge pewter tea urn grew cool and the egg and cress
sandwiches curled up, the jelly grew rock hard and
rooks in the boughs of the trees round the boarding house
cawed close of play,
you can't stay.

I was stood at dusk at the top of a long country lane,
that straightens, widens yet
slowly drops down
towards night.

Week's Worth

Monday, his steel comb (again again!) and his train ticket (which he had to re-purchase then found, two weeks later, folded between two receipts which he hadn't needed to keep); also the precise shine and shimmer of that bright, limpid turquoise glimpsed from the cliff-borne coast-road near Kas.

Tuesday, his temper with his little daughter (which smote him bitterly, bitterly, after).

Wednesday, some change that spilled out of his pocket, getting up from a very deep sofa in a café where – also (though he was never to realise it had happened here, now) – the immaculacy of his brand-new fawn trousers, spotted with cappuccino-grease spots that would, with washing, fade but never (for he was to keep them the rest of his life) ever vanish.

Thursday, the name of that jackass in Accounts, the date of his mother-in-law's birthday (again) and (he suddenly realised) the memory of what exactly he and Lorri Bennett had said each to other when they'd ridden their bikes to the Union river one hot summer's afternoon, lain in the long grass, touched one another and thought *this oh this oh this feels like being an adult!*

Friday, the notes he had painstakingly made for the big presentation next Tuesday; his last fading hopes that his wife would ever shed that stone and a half she had gained; and – for ten raging, self-hating minutes – the car keys.

Saturday, another hank of hair come away in his hairbrush (which he now wished the way of his comb – but did this hairloss signify merely everyday ageing or something more sinister of which he'd used to know the other symptoms but now couldn't, quite, whatever it might…?); either way, another few crumbs of his smashed immortality cake.

And Sunday, a few crumbs more – and the sunshine in his heart – when he looked in the mirror and saw someone gaunt, almost haggard, look right back at him; and his pride when he walked back into the bedroom and found his wife quietly weeping about the stone and a half that she just couldn't – she'd tried so hard – and she'd seen how he didn't look at her the way he once had – did that mean – what he'd felt – was now

Might they be able to conjure it back like the ring that winks up from the drain as you're desperately, vainly, trying to hook it back in?
Could that happen? Or was it…?

In her bedroom a wall away, their daughter, burrowing into the untidy pile of toys, dolls and books by her bed, had found a manky, dandruffy, steel comb.

Daddy's. He'd be so glad! She put it in pride of place on her Little Big Girl's dresser and started searching again for her dolly named Jill who was

Inasmuch

Inasmuchas
they're fresh fruit, less bruised than we;
they unsettle us.

Inasmuchas
we watch them and see what we wanted to be or perhaps
    briefly were,
those lush afternoons when the world seemed to poise in
    our grasp like a peach,
we envy them.

Inasmuchas
they either ignore or indulge us with languid regard,
declining pupillage, loyalty or even to hate us;
they treat us as though we were already
three quarters dead –
which we fear may be true.
So we hate them.

Inasmuchas they stride
over bridges we built across ditches we had to plunge
shit-smeared and drenched through;
despise them?
We do.

Inasmuchas their memories have
no shady evening dovecotes for
those pleasures whose last shreds of ripeness we suck dry;
we pity them, *listen!*
we say, *there is more to life, oh so much more!*

Are they listening though?
(Their pleasures much swifter, sweeter and sharper than
    ours.)
No. They're not.

Inasmuchas
we find our eyes smart our hearts tug when they smile,
when they smile.
Smile at us.
Inasmuchas
they grant us their trust and their time,
mining our sunken, bruised eyes for the
wisdom we lyingly claim;
inasmuchas they do, they infatuate us.
Could this brackish tank brim with cool nectar again?
Could they even – could they – love us?
The worst. That's the worst.
When that ends.

Inasmuchas while we rot,
they'll still breathe and laugh,
oh, the envy, oh
the rage!

Inasmuch as we glimpse,
just behind them, *their* nemeses
starting to grow pubic hair, to perfect mocking sniggers,
how happy we are!

Time. A crooked old man.
Moisture strains down his cracked, ruined cheeks.
Scoop him up on your shoulder

and bear him to where?
To the workhouse, the bonfire.
Why are you crying, Dad?
Because I remember, forty years gone.
As you do to yours,
I to mine.

Trying To Do Deals With Mr. C

april-
At 43, life's reasonable, but there's
this sense that she's still fumbling for some switch
to blaze the floodlights on.
She thinks she could be
happier, kinder, wiser. How, though?
She knows she can be tauter, slimmer –
'and will be! Once I've cleared this
tickle when I swallow, this grogginess
when I wake.'

august-
They had to slice her open
the better to slash and burn
the tree that grew inside her
and its seedlings. 'Now I'm clean –
and slower, yes, but who needs speed?
For years it's made me slapdash, blind!
This scar's my friend, he
tweaks and tugs, *too much, too soon,
take time!*'

december-
Now that they've blitzed and poisoned
all her miles of intricate cabling, scoured
the tunnels, swept the chambers
where the last guerrillas lurked, she's liberated –
'free! I've vomited out
all childhood dreams of
fame and beauty, what you see,
stripped down and bald,
is me!'

march-
You slowly learn that
once he sets his mark
on you, his white-gloved fist is always
but a handsbreath from your door.
He loves the bones of you, he'll not
let go, he'll not take no, 'but I'll
not beg or scream.
I'll face him down with dignity
and morphine.'

may-
It all comes down to this. All deals, all dreams.

May morning's bells have pealed.
The shimmering girls with flower-decked hair knit
hands and dance – and never sense
the gaunt, skeletal frame with plague-pit breath,
the last link in their chain,
a link that shrieks and sobs in torment as
bone scrapes and grinds on bone.
Her sharp, tight grip is slipping, slipping.
'We all. Come down. To this…'

Lunch Hour Ends At Daybreak

She'd got a night pass,
crept out for a lunch-hour;
like we used to.

Walking through our park,
picking up dropped coins,
spotting early blossoms, ducking out of showers

into the tearoom's
shell for it's been closed for years,
we crouched and shared our news – or rather mine.

We walked the maze of residential roads for
I was trying to show her where I live but
kept on coming back

to a church with people gathering
for a funeral.
It made her weep;
for the suddenness, and the children.

She'd used to swim length after shimmering length,
then hurry back to work –
wet hair, dried-up sandwich.

I'm teaching swimming now, she said,
through mercury, through crystal –
in the nude!

Which made me think of the other
way we'd used to fumbling-
frenziedly spend lunch-hours.

I asked if maybe – *what?!* she frowned,
you're surely not THAT kind of perve?
And yet she blushed, looked pleased and I thought *yes!*
Yes! Still!

I set the timer on my camera,
held her hand quite lightly,
recalling how she'd used to squirm away.

Our hour had slipped, slid, guttered
down, she said *please don't forget me…*
even if I can't get away again?

My photograph, of course, was just
park railings, a few lilies.
Wasn't even any sign of me.

My bedroom; daylight's first grey and
soft weeping, which I think
must have been me.

Yet no regrets for her sweet visit,
grief's a price I gladly pay
to be that young and that in love
for a few seconds,
again.

Bequest

On the first perfect dawn
after my death-day,
wake yourself early – you'll
need no alarm.
Tread softly through your garden,
breathe its perfumes, sip its birdsong
and wash your eyes with dew.
There'll be stillness, something
waiting, there'll be sunbeams melting mist.
There will be buds that gently ripple into
scarlet, snow and gold.
And is all this juice
just death's digestion? Yes!
And so, my love, are you,
come stretch your flesh-robed fingers out,
pluck the dense, bright air.
Remember how my soft touch felt?
It's here, it's here!

On the first fine weekend
after my death-day,
motor through the peaks –
you'll have to
map-read for yourself.
You'll find that cottage, by a stream,
we stayed – go in, love, rest till dark then,
if you switch off all the lights and music, step outside –
then stop.
You'll feel the night close up around you,
sparkling waters rill and purl as
time; breathes; out.

Now, wait till you are wholly swallowed,
wait – wait…
Now! Look up!
At the dazzle of a million furnaces
incinerating all we knew.
I'm not out there,
my only home's
in you, in you!

And what of every other day
after my death day?
Stumbling through the din and chaos,
your wings torn by neglect, your
beauty dulled with pain.
No garden and no starlit night.
What have I for you, now?
Reflections in a crowd.
Other eyes as green but fresher;
tiny, pointless acts of kindness;
someone, grieving, comforted,
if only for an hour.
Tiny drops of honesty,
little shreds of care – *there,*
in the dark heart of your grey world,
in the hour of your despair,
the truth that you and I
possessed's
around you –
everywhere!

Life After Life After Death

When they buried her,
it was a rain-whipped daybreak,
the bare trees crouched and wept.
There'd been fever in the settlement,
Jet was the first adult to die.
They mixed a paste of ashes, smeared
their clothes, their cheeks, their eyes, their hair.
They ripped their flesh with fingernails,
used filthied brooms to scourge grief free.

Jet's dulled eyes gazed up through her father.
Is here? this? my betrothal bed?
He sealed each eye with silver coin,
he kissed her marble brow.
It froze his lips.

They brimmed a glass with sweetened wine.
A plate was spread with cakes.
Her finest silks, a fragrant wreath
as pillow, then they sealed her in.
And then they bore her to the graveside
as the horns brayed Hail! Death's might!
A gleam of sunbright briefly lit
the thud and spread of soil.

She goes! We mourn!
But gone, we must forget
we ever grieved.
Until we let her pass from us,
her long blind journey to the sun
cannot even
commence.

When she awoke,
Jet was alone and it was dark
but there was noise, such thunderous noise!
There had been piercing pain and such cracked thirst
or were those merely dreams?
And still the splintering, shattering, something
cracking round her like a shell.
Terror at her fingertips, yet she was calm as grass –
then pain, a thread of screaming pain,
first wafer thin and coffin lid shaped,
broader soon with every new crack,
licking up the chamber's blackness,
searing any vision blank and
scorching spirit clean.
So clean!

There were words she had to say, she had been
taught them, now she stammered.
'By Jupiter and by the Christ,' she croaked, she
gasped, 'where is my mother?
Let her be my guide here.
For I would speak to her.'

Close by, the sun's breath shimmered upon harp-strings,
     swelled and sighed.
Gentle hands were lifting her,
and slotting her into a breeze, which gently rocked
and dipped
towards a plaintive melody,
her mother's voice!

Jet wept.
And whose sweet laughter bubbling
beneath? Her little brother's!
Jet had no fear as liquid sucked around,
above and through her.
A pool so warm, so dense and spiced,
the rags she wore of silk and flesh slipped off
and melted, pungence filled her
mouth, her nostrils, drank her.
Like mist at dawn, her memories span
and shredded, while their frail bright seeds
distilled through woodland herbs and flowers
that softly breathed them out.

Yet these things too were only dreams
flickering through the restless night
of instants as Jet's brainstem died,
of centuries as she lay.
Outside her cell, the settlement
was torn down, pasted back up, burnt
then dreamed anew and stitched afresh, .
mere inches from her head.
Faint rumours of this, whispers, sighs,
leaking through the soil,
as acorns split and one in thousands grew
to spreading treehood,
as centuries rolled and empires unrolled,
mouldering down to puddles.

Towards morning, mighty blasts, long groans
and something shifted, wet clay dribbled
through a crack and filled her long-dry glass.

As sixty more years passed, the earth span louder,
swelling every year,
it swarmed in through the womb of dirt,
a virus called the future.

When they resurrected Jet,
mighty steel hands gripped her bed.
Their music was the deathscream of a God
whose breath was fire.
Bladed fingernails slit her shell
then prised and spread and cracked it.
Slices of a sun blazed through and
glorified her skull.
The coffin lid was hoisted clear and
seven arc lights poured out heat
as seven angels, burning bright in overalls and masks,
advanced with probes and blades and forceps,
picked at Jet so tenderly
as piece by drying piece,
by dusty speck of chestnut hair by
filigree of silk,
by microbe trace of what had killed her and fragment of
    her spine,
they stripped and brushed her cleaner,
more beautiful and nuder
than any lover could.

Though God may wash each fragment
of our carcasses in ichor
then like a jigsaw slot us back together
still he can't
re-awake what rot has touched or
sprout flesh back on bone.

They sealed Jet in that crystal casket
our breath fogs up as we gaze down,
her long night's journey to the light
is ended but she cannot wake,
we flick our jaded eyes
from cranium to rib-cage down to metatarsal bones
to the face-mould from her skull which
gazes steadily back at us.
Her cobalt eyes and pensive jaw
compress a little tighter
and pierce our butter flesh.
She watches as *our* bone-frames flex and
promenade the galleries,
dawdle in the refectory
then quickly down the rubbish chute
to incinerate or slime,
where the tossing and turning of eternity begins.
And they'll begin much sooner than you think,
sighs Jet's calm mask –
and she should know.

Her tight, alert face fascinates
my upper backbones closer closer,
kiss her on the forehead – ah!
It chills my dusty lips.
A bolt of lightning splits my grinding brain
and now I know!

That I have never forgotten you,
daughter, springbud, wildflower, heart.
Though our souls have migrated,
though bodies have been smelted, melted down
and forged again.

Centuries on I kiss your mask
above a crystal shrine,
whose guardians seize my shoulders, *hold on mate!*
and haul me back again
into a world so strange
and yet erected on our bones
where the strangest ancient memories
bubble up like sulphur and
evaporate, Jet...

So that again I lose you,
child I mourned when I wore other skin.
And are you waiting in the darkness for the tunnel and
    light again?
Or have you breathed and died again, I missed you
by a century or a continent, sweet Jet?
Or dwell we in this urgent city, passing daily in some
    crowd,
eyes never meeting? Oh!
All I can pray is
you still bear the seed
of having been loved
and pass that seed on, down
these lives lived after death
before we die.

PART TWO : LIFE

Then, Years Later, I Met Him Again

At a party; well, it
would be, wouldn't it?
Such smarm! He'd forgotten
he'd cheated and betrayed me.
They do that, kid themselves that,
because they're the stars in those movies
that play in their heads,
it's you who's shabby
if you don't forgive them,
don't offer yourself for seduction all over again.

And damn my soul, I responded.
Hearty handshake, ripe smile.

As the drink flowed, shame
rose up my gorge.
He was so shiny and polished, and I?
Just a petty scratch on the world,
barely noticeable.

I followed him into the toilets.
A few cutting words?
Headlock and smash him
against the glazed tiles?
'Good do, eh?' he grinned.

I turned, all innocence, still
urinating, across up and down his
trousers, 'oh, I'm sorry!'
and could almost have forgiven him

if he'd taken it, rather than –
after those few frozen instants of shock –
jumping back in disgust.
Him! At me!

'People don't forget,' I smiled,
'everybody hated you, still do,
I expect.' Turning back
to the urinal, to zip myself up.

'Wha – what's your problem?' he wanted
to punch me, for someone
in his position, not wise.
So his fist dropped and
I pressed a little money
into it, 'here.
Can't leave you to pay for
cleaning up your mess,
can we?'

No bones or teeth had been
broken, just a spatter of fairly
quick-drying stains, although
he didn't see it quite that way.
'You're – sick!'

Indeed. But unbowed.
And with style.
All that's left, sometimes.

She Refuses to Play Pass the Parcel

What could Scar do
when the boy she fancied
left her in the lurch
on a dripping dreary
Sunday aftergloom?

And a speeding-past car splashed road-puddle over her.
And scuttling home, sopping-skirt, streaming hair, sobbing,
passers-by mocked her – *scarecrow! slapper!* –
what could she, what should she do?

Stone through his window?
V-sign at them?
No, things might get rough – might get violent.
You could squat on the poison
then spit it on
to the next one who dared to cross you.
Tempting to imagine the shock and awe on their
flaccid Monday-morn faces!

Like
watching herself from a tower and
the self she was watching was
striding an ancient square,
running her fingers up and down, up and down
something sharp, bright, cruel.

As bells began tolling and crows came billowing out of the
evening sun.
a someone came skipping across the square

and the self she was watching
lunged.

But the writhing one on the flagstones looked
strangely like Scarlett, too.
Were we passing pain round like a parcel in
ten thousand simultaneous games
with the blame always somebody's else?
But how far back would you go?
Who had shafted the boy who had just shafted her?
And who them? And how quickly a whole chain uncoiled
    that
could surely be winched back if only
one soul that was fed with betrayals, foul words
could resist the vomit-back,
could digest the sawdust and dung
into just so much kindness and care, handed on
to the next fellow pilgrims she passed?

And might this reverse gulf-streams, break gravity's pull –
a.k.a. stop us bruising each other,
bruises spreading each time we cross paths?

Crazy thoughts with a nag-nagging pull
as her mousy hair dried in clumps
and her eye-shadow ran in zombie zags,
she'd slogged the four miles home.

Where the warm sweet scent of the Polish bakery
was drifting up her street.
Where the lads from next door were booting a football
through the dusk and dreich.

Tha' looks like a tramp, Scar! The fat one said soft,
the scrawny one chuckled and stared,
ball trapped under his foot.
They'd expect no less than a vicious reply spat
to haul them low as her –
she paused, she thought, then –
Gi' us a kick, then!
She thrashed it, the fat one spreadeagled –
Oh saved! She clapped his shoulder
and felt him glow – almost smile –
felt something unclench, shift, rise and snap
back deep inside her chest.

Not necessarily forgiveness –
Scar sat chewing egg on toast…
And not that she'd ever forget standing petrified on the
     cinema steps,
for the boy who'd instead sent the text she was staring at –
     over bitch piss off byee…
To live in a world where this and much worse –
and this was dreadful enough and so
what must the worst be like? –
kept happening every day…

She took a long draught of tea.
One – not to ever play pass the parcel
back or across or on…
And two – about trying to pass down the line
as much tenderness as you'd felt pain;
right?
She piled crocks into the sink
Mum was calling her *Corrie's on! Scar!*

57

Brows creased, her hair wild and jagged,
eyes narrowed into a frown,
just this girl, this Scarlett Jade Smith who was pondering
shaking the world upside down.

Marina

Two tall and slender glasses,
one half-drunk and lipstick-smeared,
the other dry as hope.

A pair of high heels,
one snapped off,
strewn across the hallway.

Taut lace thong
crumpled by the door.

On the sofa,
gloss and flashy magazine,
opened at a page where beautiful women in beautiful
    clothes with
painted faces
gaze at us with vacancy.

Gold and purple basket for
even waste, she hoped, would be – what?
Elegant.
Now slowly slowly filling with
damp tissues that mascara
tears have bled on.

Push the magazine off.
Sprawl across the sofa like a dog
side-swiped by a car door,
naked, feel the bruising gather and swell.
Nothing fatal. Nothing fatal.

Grey wet November day
blown in on the Humber.
Such a silly little bitch

who, like some hero,
never will
stop trying.

At Copps Hill

There's one small corner of this racing, screaming city,
between the markets and the freeway, staring
down upon the docks.

Bounded by an ancient wall, shrouded by embracing trees,
green with grass and fertilised by bone,
this must not change although the rest
metamorphose faster
every year.

Glorious summer sunsets across the bay,
we climb above the swirl of
lead and sweat and caffeine,
with bread and fruit and wine amongst your graves
we sit and feast.

Ain't sure whether to bless you or to curse you;
see what your dreams and pride have brought us to.

Your small, worm-eaten, beautiful
corner of our minds.

English Girl

She's a late summer afternoon.
So late it's almost evening,
or autumn.
Sunshine in her eyes and shadows on her back.
A little breeze.

She's gripping a hot air balloon
that skips and scrapes along the cliff then
Out! – above the sands, above
the galloping horses, shrimping children,
huge dusk ocean's gaping mouth,
wherever waits, whatever's there – even
drowning?

Splashes her face with fizz-chilled tonic,
dabs her cleavage with lemon.
Feels gin start to prowl around her stomach
like a tiger, like a fuse
for making laughter, love
or rage.

And her upper arms, bare, stun me.
Bone under muscle under tight tanned
skin under fine soft down.
Shaping and shading the slopes, twists, curves, the
ledge to the tree of her throat.
Lovelier than mountains at sunset –
scree-slip precipice-plunge.

But she's rourke's drift, too.
Her forward prod
to stub the fierce firecrackers out,
twelve overs left to bat to snatch
a draw from out the jaws of
cemetery, eternity –
play! Play up! And play the game!
In maiden white over
clinging lycra she
drives the reaper wicketless
from the field.

Nearby the scented stocks and blooms and
herbs that wriggle and wind and spread
between the giggling sunbeams,
amongst the shadowing tombstones,
are whispering their riddles
to the bees.

She's dead a hundred million times and
yet she's not yet born and yet
you may watch this evening
her laughing by the gate;
or strolling pensive by the byre or,
as she passes, singing and,
though voice and face and tune may change,
her haunting never ends;
her song remains the
same
English girl's.

Naomi Watts at the Taormina Film Festival

In the broken amphitheatre,
the shades slide through her,
gibbering of duty, betrayal, revenge,
she drinks their pain,
their parched lips taste peace,
the Gods died yet
Drama still heals.
Perched on the cracked marble seats, she's a little girl
clap-clap-hurrahing with sore hands
this ravishing world:
a curtain of flame-basted eggshell-blue air,
back of the stage and temple;
fifty miles of crinkled shoreline
and a cool swim in every calm bay.

The shimmering paparazzi pasta,
the drizzled cheese and oil-drenched tomatoes
even the ripe golden wine;
though she savours them all with the same slow
   intentness she listens,
they're not her.

Whereas Etna's snow-ring,
its spherical perfect its
dark and whispering mouth
scalding magma gripped tight
as her breasts by the little white
dress that her quiver-smile kindles –

She is not hauling her man from an abyss of heroin
nor her child from leukaemia
nor thwarting a madman –
whose goons swagger crab-wise from the size of their uzis
and whose babes flaunt bikinis (but none quite as skimpily
    flattering as
hers) – from world domination.

She is sun dripping through frangipani and shattering.
She is wave-crack and foam-sighing ebb.
Etna's roar, scorch and petrification's
her merciless rage.
She's the soft haunted breeze
through your hair.

Where are the writer, director, first camera,
best boy and sparks
to immortalise her
while her candle is flaming high?
Perhaps – almost certainly –
they will never quite
all coincide.

Which makes today and its sense of what might –
in a magical place on an afternoon floating a –
shreds of her devastating dragonfly prime –
precious so
very precious.

First Day

I watch her skip
across the playground dismissing
me an impatient little twitch
of her fingers and mouth
I'm irrelevant
already she's always
lunging grabbing
jumping at tomorrow.
Still
I have to stand sentinel
till she vanishes into
her other world she
might turn her head one day to
find me gone and –
what?
Realise that
she's not as brave
as she and I pretend?

Her face – tearwet or frighted –
haunts me through the day
I want to stride in –
Who's been bullying my girl? –
Terrifying for five year olds.
Stupid too when I recall
me as a child how mortified
by my dad fighting my wars.

Back at the schoolyard
glimpse her through a window
waves to me but crossly and
shakes her head I
think that underneath she's
glad to see I've
bothered to turn up
even though she chatters to new friends
the whole way home
ignores me.

She's kidding herself she doesn't need me
aren't I?

After Night Shift

'smostly the din.
Think a thousand skillets and pans
collidin', churnin' all night.

Tries to shake it outa his head,
pulls at the first sweet cigarette of –
ah! It steadies the carpark under his feet.

'sgot a little, beat-up open-top,
used to be a bottle of rye in the glove-box
till that got a little too needful.

Such a beautiful mornin',
flamin' east sky, air fit to wash with.
He accelerates onto the backroad.

Then a track, tumblin' off to the waterfront,
sold for a million but no bricks or diggers yet.
Private – keep out! Yeah, like hell.

Estuary runnin', ribbons of mist,
trees close 'n' tall with birdsong pourin' and
that screech in his head's hushed at last.

A crack, a rustle – a bear? Shit,
no!

He freezes and out the corner of his eye spies –
gently croppin' then
suddenly freezin' –
a deer!

And, before he can stir, the drill of a woodpecker
pierces his heart and
time splinters.

Our war has burnt and swallowed our children!
Our president shot! To death!
Our nation is under attack!
We are all of us nothing! Nothing!

Men have come here, men unlike him, so
like him in coming for centuries at
daybreak and nightfall to
peer 'cross the mile-wide river,
searchin'.

Deer tosses her head.
Woodpecker suddenly ceases
its hypnotic throb.
His cigarette butt
arcs into water,
hisses and vanishes
like he will – he turns away thinkin'

Life, if you can
grab as it runs,
still real fine.
But you gotta grab.

And here's to those to come.
All those men and those women
yet to come.

Aurelia's Garden

There's an overgrown path between roots that trip, beneath
    boughs that drip,
on a sun-showery evening in springtime.

Where the woodland ends, meadows billow and plunge,
    under wind, over wold,
but first you must pass the villa,

where fresh springs ooze from a tangle of wild flowers
that once was Aurelia's garden.

Facades have crumbled, colonnades rubbled, the ceilings
    have sagged, fallen in.
Grime and grit crust the mosaic
of Apollo borne by a dolphin.

And beneath the shrine to the little house Gods and the
    sprites of spring and wood
is a deep, shivering crack.
Any hand reaching in will touch parchment.

Yellowed, cobwebbed and mouse-dropping-speckled,
it powders to dust at your fingertip.

So you have to imagine the story it tells of a heat-soaked,
    deserted farmhouse
by a lake in the Tuscan hills.

Where under an altar to Him they call Christ, an ingenious
   hidden shelf holds
a heap of dried wildflower seeds
and a tightly red-ribboned silk scroll,

which bears a poem which sighs for a land of poppies,
   rainbows and mist,
of shimmering sunsets in spring
and a haunted villa by woods.

Your past will leak into your future,
whose shadows darkened your past.
You hear each call to other
over your ever-sliding *now*
as, dappled, damp-stained yet glowing,
you walk out, one spring evening, singing

of a man who writes to speak to the heart
of a woman who isn't yet born;
of a woman who feels the breath on her cheek
of a dead man, of this man, and that

woman, Aurelia, is you.

How to Behave When You Lose It

for Hull Resource Centre – CRO side

Don't sniffle, grovel, plead or weep.
Don't press the suicide or nuclear buttons.
Say your piece straight and don't fret
how you'll sound for your sad heart will give you a voice,
though a hushed and a creaking one, maybe.
Smile – can you? Narrowing your eyes as you
try to recall just how good, oh how
wonderfully good this has been.
Don't beg for a day more – an
hour – one minute – ten seconds!
The fruit has begun to decay.
It will only get bitterer now
on your lips. It's the end. It's the end. It's the end.
You've been lucky to have this so long.
May you know it again but –
and I know this is tough but, through
gritted teeth, *really!* It's true –
far more important, may those
who've been unlucky so far,
may they know a time just as bright, just as sweet,
as this was,
though too briefly, for you.

Eighteen in 1972

Fumbles to move his chair closer.
Knocking the light café table and
slopping her coffee.
Oh yeah, definitely me!

Looked so young, didn't I?
Something in that
grin almost desperate?
Trying to submerge myself in her.
Trying to convince her to love me.
Embarrassing fool!

That *I'm beautiful* simper
and *can't we be friends?* nervous smile as
she tries to sober his enthusiasms up, she's a princess?
A bitch! Come on, glance
over here at my grey head, these
sour eyes that have drilled back through decades to watch
    you, girl –
listen to me!

That charming father of yours will die
choking –
cancer, of course!
And your elegant mother?
Even their money can't pay off despair, I see
overdose, breakdown –
and, oh, most embarrassing,
the gin!

This rage I never let myself show surges
up my throat but
not spoken, not spoken, but so nearly spoken as
sat in this corner,
pretending I'm not watching,
I am watching –

her frowning and stroking his hands for
there's just not that spark, though you're funny and
fun to be with, I don't like you like that,
and besides,
yes, besides there is somebody else.
Him trying to slide his fingers in between
her fingers and
trying to laugh off her brush-off, that elegant *piss-off!*
as, cracked and callow, stubborn and brave,
a lifetime's vocation as *friend* never *passion*
begins on that March afternoon in that chintzy café
(now buried under a car park).
And suddenly I find my face wet.

Are you alright, sir?
Can we help?

Look up – that impossibly smooth face, that
silly posh voice I long ago jettisoned and I
have no memory of all of this happening –
but, of course, from now on, I might!
Their blushes of earnest embarrassment are
oh yeah, definitely Sally and me!

So I speak in my soft classless voice of now, say *it's*
alright, just memories, I'm
fine now, you're
both of you very kind but
you mustn't mind me, carry on.

Then I pick up and sip my decades-stale coffee,
nibble my cobweb éclair as
my last twitch of anger curdles to shame.
To have broken the first rule of time travel!
Not to show yourself up to your
young self in front of his girlfriend;
not that she is so it
probably doesn't count, eh Sally?
Who can't drag her lovely eyes from me,
Glancing from me to me, frowning and biting her lip and
she's – typically – almost but *not* comprehending while
he? He is back to his laughable efforts to
make her smile bloom like the fool's gold
which he has no need of if
only he knew how much
treasure he holds.

Not Sally nor those other Sallies on whom he – I – wasted
so much young man's precious green time but
his gentleness and
inextinguishable hope.

He would find better uses to put them to.

Bearing Witness

Launching our paper planes
down the stairwell
into darkness.

Taking a walk
when you've been sick
(or remember you're dying).
It's spring and
the birdsong the tight buds the breeze the taste
of start again swallow and smile.

Glimpsing the silver spokes hurtling past
to leave you behind.
Sticking your grainy walking-stick into 'em.
Oh calamity!

The ground is full of the young and unwilling
who nevertheless had to pass.
We tread on their heads every day.
Much worse to betray them
by time-wasting.

The sun slips round the manor house
like an assassin.
The morning-room windows are
cold now.

Skimming stones over the deep mere.
Truth-telling.

Working at happiness
like a master-carpenter who
turns a block to
a delicate, intricate carved toy
a child can love
and pass on
                and pass on
                        and pass on.

Waiting. Watching. Listening.
Then launching our paper planes
down the stairwell and
into darkness.

Jackets 'n' Skins

Vinegar-soaked chips were for waltzing her home after
    ten or twelve pints...
Skewering roasties with her parents' posh Sunday
    cutlery...
And tender charlottes drizzled with pepper and oil
for dinner parties on the patio...

But what are baked potatoes for?

His Gran had served them charred crisp,
fluffy inside and golden with butter and love –
and cheese and beans too, if she'd won on the horses.

He finds himself lately, frequently baking potatoes,
late home from the office to a cold, silent house.
Softened up in the microwave
then into the oven and blasted into submission –
but never as tasty as
he recalls or expects,
nor as comforting ate on your own without grandma's –
or for that matter anyone's –
eyes dancing *eat it all up, it'll*
warm you all the way down!

See, he'd always wanted everything *now!*
Grabbed stuff, dolloped on loads and
then ate it too fast.
Burnt lips and, afterwards, indigestion.
And an empty plate in an empty house to stare at
all evening long.

Walks a lot, now, for hours and miles, through the rain.
One day, steps through the fog and the anthracite smoke
into a small café with a greasy plasticate menu
with *spuds in their skins*.
Wouldn't have chosen it had there been
anything else even remotely to savour.
A long wait, he
wouldn't have put up with but
where else? What else? And anyway,
why the hell not?
His mind drifting back to the charlottes and roasties and chips,
to how life was before.
His hunger dully stirring.

The she brought it out to his table, steaming and bubbling and
    soaked and scented with
butter and salt, cheese and sauce.
She said *here, get that down you, then, love and*
cheer up, it's what proves God exists, this –
and wants us to be replete
if we can't be happy!

And,
d'you know what?
She was right.
Even him
and right down to the very last mouthful.
Could have eaten another.
But knew how important it was that he didn't.
At any rate, not today.
He had the whole of the rest of his life
to work up an appetite
again.

We Fought

We saw star-peppered heaven and crystal moon –
and crimson mist coating the tail-gunner's turret;
and dark-charred meat in the pilot's seat
we saw.

We heard voices on our frequency
screaming *we're going down!* for
transmission tends to scramble – and
sobbing and pleading with God or for Mum.
With relief it's not you –
and guilt that it's not
scraping you raw –
you listen.

We learnt ducking, weaving and hairline adjustments.
Then we raced over, stopped, dropped tanks full of fire
and pissed back even faster.
For that was what truly we'd learnt –
and that you fight for civilisation
by incinerating children
and, strange to say, that it works.
Forty fried kids for one torched mate?
Too few. Too soft. No deal.

And that mates, your mates are all you can trust for
they, they alone, understand your dark laughter as,
cramming your tongue and your soul down tonight's
     cheap girl's throat,
with that casual flick of your wrist,
you slop out the heady wine –

and that hopes and plans and fear are tourniquets
cutting off blood to the brain;
that labelling your forehead *provisionally dead*
is the likeliest way to survive –
and that heaven is sunrise
over an empty bay,
tide flooding in and
all engines singing and
clean bright sheets ahead.

And hell?
Dying slowly
in a country that hasn't a glimmering clue
what you killed in yourself when
you roasted your fleecy white soul into stinking, cracked
    leather.
And it won't grow back.
Better, much better leave now,
before they sell what we die for
for pennies…

…retrieved our bikes from the stables and
cycling back over the dunes
towards base it was 4 maybe 5 a.m.
whisky, exhaustion tangling our legs and our chains until
Stan fell off into a dyke Jack and Robbie collided
dropping the last of the water of life seeping into the sand as
we heard on the dawn breeze the scream
of a gull the bark of a fox and
away to the east a low cry that
chilled us sobered us
cry of a bomber coming in on one engine and too little fuel

and – now we could glimpse it –
too low!

Swaying in limping home
struggling to hold height and skim those last miles.
Haemorrhaging fuel and smoke.

We were motionless till
it roared past fifty feet overhead that
unlocked us we screamed and waved gestured them in –
God knows they knew the way!
Ran throwing bikes down
we ran!
It's M! M for Mother!
You bastards you jammy sod bastards!
Shot up and blasted but crawling back home –
while a couple miles inland the
sirens and klaxons and screaming of tyres and sergeants
the whole bloody base was erupting while
here on the dunes
we were screaming like madmen *c'mon chaps!*
Don't bugger-up now when you're so nearly home!
Bring her in, slot her down
sweet and true!

Could they see us, hear us?
No matter,
we were screaming for us who, tonight or
tomorrow or next week would be as they now were
or worse.
C'mon chaps!

Cheering a crew of probably dying
probable woman- and child-killers back to the starred prize of
burning to death on the runway or else
being spared yet again so's to do it all over again.
Yet that dawn on those dunes
was the most alive most
vivid tenderest hour
of my life.
Everything since a mere shadow.

And I hope that you can't understand that my child.
Though it might after all these years
help you to understand me.

Pray

Say that the summer had never ended,
say we could have wandered on a few miles
further east each day,
tracing the rim of that whispering sea,
pacing, racing the sun.

Say that our sun had never been smudged
and shrouded by English skies.

Say that those sparks flaring up from that fire
on that beach where we feasted on aubergine, bread,
 cheese and wine –

That those sparks were still vaulting
into pitch black heaven,
whose dazzling congregation
humming down upon us –

Say that those sparks, that pine wood, that summer
had never consumed themselves.

Say that your fingers still warm flesh in mine,
your lips still moist at my ear and saying this –

Say this.
Please say it.
Please.